TEACH YOURSELF TO PLAY

GUITAR SCALES

by Steve Gorenberg

Don't delay, start today!

This book provides a quick, effective, uncomplicated, and practical method to playing guitar scales. Get started right away and learn at your own pace in the comfort of your home.

To access audio visit:
www.halleonard.com/mylibrary

2219-8125-2681-2316

Other *Teach Yourself to Play Guitar* books

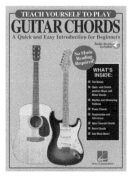

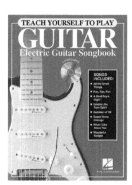

00144128   00696029   00699791

ISBN 978-1-4950-6469-2

HAL•LEONARD®
CORPORATION
7777 W. BLUEMOUND RD. P.O. BOX 13819 MILWAUKEE, WI 53213

In Australia Contact:
Hal Leonard Australia Pty. Ltd.
4 Lentara Court
Cheltenham, Victoria, 3192 Australia
Email: ausadmin@halleonard.com.au

Visit Hal Leonard Online at
www.halleonard.com

Introduction

Congratulations on your decision to learn guitar scales! Scales form the foundation for all melody, riffs, and solos on the guitar. *Teach Yourself to Play Guitar Scales* is an excellent place to begin, whether you've played a musical instrument before or not. This book doesn't require you to have any prior musical experience; you'll be able to start playing right away, without having to learn how to read traditional music. The examples in this book are all presented in an easy-to-follow system designed specifically for beginner guitar.

This book begins with some basic guitar knowledge, the parts of the guitar, how to tune, how to hold the guitar, and how to read scale diagrams and tablature—just the very basics to get you started. Then we'll dive right into the playing! As you progress through the book, you'll learn the notes on the guitar and how to play major and minor scales, pentatonic scales, and blues scales, along with a simple rhythmic notation system, all shown without traditional music notation. Also included are scale patterns and exercises to help you master guitar scales and picking, all with the help of the recorded tracks so you can hear exactly how everything should sound.

The objective is to help you master the scales at your own pace. Be patient and take your time in the beginning, reviewing each example to make sure that you've got it down before moving on. Once you've learned the beginning major and minor scales and can play them smoothly, you'll be well on your way. Then we'll continue with scale patterns, pentatonic scales, and two- and three-octave scales—all without having to read music or learn a lot of theory. By the time you get through this book, you'll be equipped with the knowledge you need to continue learning and growing as a guitarist long after you've mastered everything presented here. Most of all, go have fun!

Table of Contents

Chapter 1
Getting Started

Tuning

The strings on the guitar are tuned in order from the lowest-sounding (thickest) string to the highest-sounding (thinnest) string. The lowness or highness of a note is called *pitch*. The six guitar strings are tuned to specific pitches when played *open* (no fingers pressing them down). In order, from lowest to highest, the pitches of the open strings are: E, A, D, G, B, and E. The highest-sounding (thinnest) string is referred to as the 1st string; the lowest-sounding (thickest) string is referred to as the 6th string.

TRACK 01

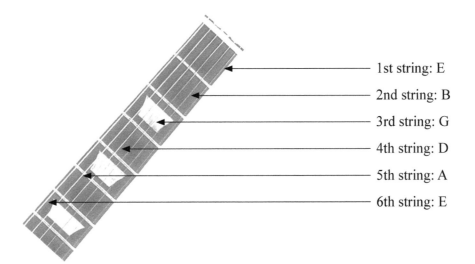

1st string: E
2nd string: B
3rd string: G
4th string: D
5th string: A
6th string: E

Scale Diagrams

Scales are taught in this book using graphic representations of the fretboard called *scale diagrams*. The horizontal lines in the diagrams represent the strings; the vertical lines represent the frets. The thick vertical line at the left of the diagram represents the nut. Scale diagrams visually correspond to the guitar as if you laid the guitar flat on your lap, with the strings facing up.

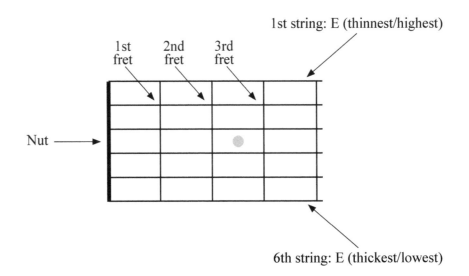

1st string: E (thinnest/highest)

1st fret   2nd fret   3rd fret

Nut

6th string: E (thickest/lowest)

Black or white dots are placed on the scale diagrams to indicate the fretted (pressed down) notes, and the numbers in the dots represent which fingers to use to fret the notes. A number is assigned to each finger of your left hand: 1 = index, 2 = middle, 3 = ring, 4 = pinky.

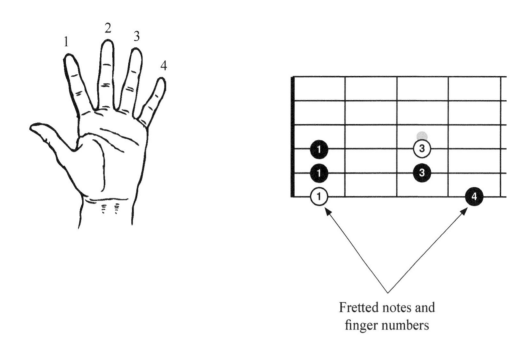

Fretted notes and
finger numbers

Tablature

Tablature (or *tab*) is another system for notating guitar music without using traditional notes. A tab staff consists of six horizontal lines, each representing a string on the guitar. The lowest line represents the lowest-pitched string (6th string), and the highest line represents the highest-pitched string (1st string). The numbers placed on the string lines refer to fret numbers on the guitar. If a "0" is used, it means the string should be played open (not fretted). If an "X" is used, then the string should be muted. Chords are represented in tab by stacking the numbers on top of each other.

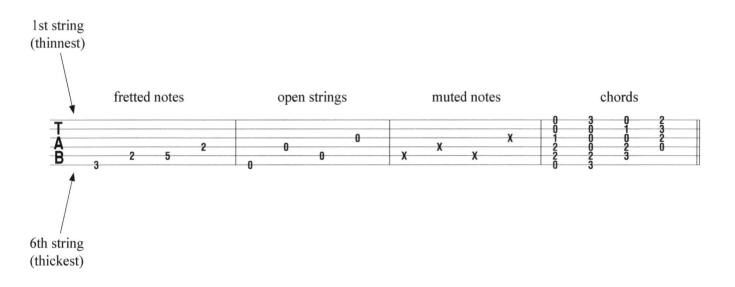

1st string
(thinnest)

6th string
(thickest)

Left-hand Position

Keep your left hand relaxed and your fingers arched. The first joint of your thumb and your fingertips are the only parts of your hand that should be touching the guitar. Avoid gripping the neck like a baseball bat (your palm should not be touching the guitar neck).

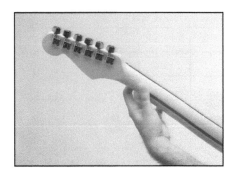

Place the first joint of your thumb
on the back of the guitar neck.

Curl your fingers so that only your
fingertips are touching the strings.

Holding the Pick

Hold the pick in your right hand by gripping it firmly between your thumb and first finger. Keep the rest of your hand relaxed and your fingers slightly curved and out of the way. You can pick the strings in a downward motion using a *downstroke*, or in an upward motion using an *upstroke*. Most of the time, you'll be combining the two in an alternating down-up-down-up motion. While picking single notes, the motion should come from your wrist. While strumming chords, keep your wrist straight and let the motion come from your elbow.

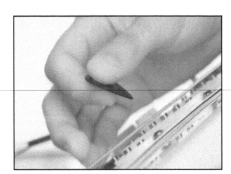

Many exercises in this book will include a series of symbols above the tab to indicate downstrokes and upstrokes.

Downstroke   Upstroke

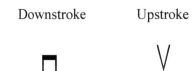

Chapter 2
The C Major Scale

The major scale forms the foundation of most other scales and chords in Western music. The notes are famously showcased in the song "Do-Re-Mi" from *The Sound of Music*.

The musical alphabet utilizes the letters A through G. If you count up from C to C in the musical alphabet (C–D–E–F–G–A–B–C), you'll have the notes of the C major scale. The first note of the scale, C, is called the *tonic* (also known as the *root note*); this is the note that gives the scale its letter name. C major is a good key to start with because it's unique in that it contains all *natural notes* (no sharps or flats). The distance from the first C to the next higher or lower C in the musical alphabet is called an *octave*.

Below is one octave of the C major scale, beginning on the note C at the third fret of the fifth string. The scale is shown in tab and also with a scale diagram. The root notes, C, are indicated with white dots in the diagram; the rest of the notes in the scale are shown with black dots. Fret the notes with the finger numbers indicated on the diagram and underneath the tab staff. Play through the scale slowly, making sure to get a clean tone for each note. Be sure your hands are positioned properly (as shown in the previous chapter).

C Major Scale

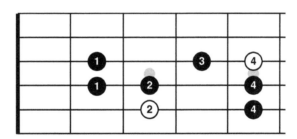

TRACK 02

Now play through the notes of the scale in reverse, or *descending* order. Here it is in tab, with the fingering indicated under the staff.

TRACK 03

Now let's play through the scale continuously, ascending and descending. As with all scales, it's important for you to be equally comfortable playing the scale in both directions.

TRACK 04

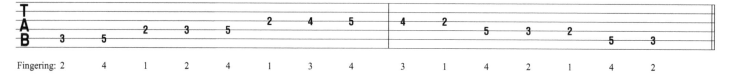

Here are a few exercises that will help you to memorize the scale. This first example breaks down the scale to focus on the notes on each individual string. Start slowly, playing through the notes at an even, steady speed to produce a smooth, clean tone.

TRACK 05

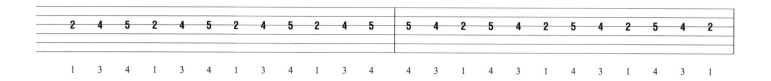

It's usually a good idea to employ alternate picking when practicing scales and exercises in order to build speed and good technique. The next example includes the picking symbols that were discussed in the previous chapter. In this exercise, play the scale ascending and descending, picking each note twice (down-up, down-up, etc.). Play this example continuously at a smooth, even speed.

TRACK 06

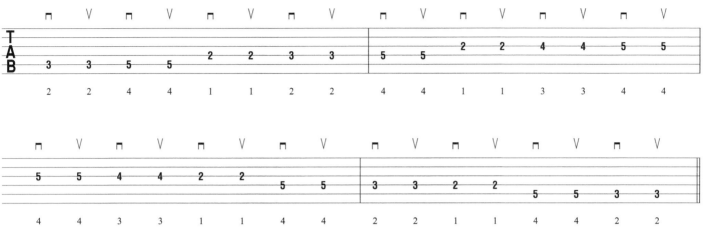

Now try ascending and descending the regular C major scale, using alternate picking as shown below.

Here's a popular scale pattern exercise that plays through one-octave of the C major scale in groups of three notes. Beginning on the root note, ascend three notes of the scale, then play the second note of the scale and ascend three more notes, continuing in this fashion until you reach the octave. The second line of tablature shows the pattern descending from the octave C in reverse order. Play steadily through the exercise without pausing between the notes. Once you've got the pattern worked out, apply alternate picking.

TRACK 07

Chapter 3
The A Minor Scale

Another essential scale used in all styles of music is the minor scale. Compared to the major scale, the minor scale has a dark, or melancholy, characteristic. Western music has incorporated a few altered versions of the minor scale, but for this lesson, we'll focus on the original and most popular version, the *natural minor* scale—also referred to as simply the "minor scale."

Like the C major scale, the A minor scale also contains only natural notes (no sharps or flats). By playing through the notes of the musical alphabet, from A to A, you'll have the A minor scale.

Below is one octave of the A minor scale, beginning on the note A at the fifth fret of the sixth string. The scale is shown in tab and also with a scale diagram. Notice the "5 fr." indicator located below the diagram. This indicates that the first area of the diagram corresponds to the fifth fret on the guitar. The root notes, A, have been indicated with white dots in the diagram; the rest of the notes in the scale are shown with black dots.

A Minor Scale

TRACK 08

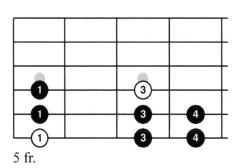

5 fr.

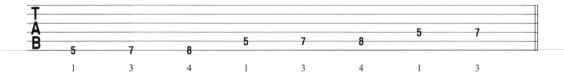

Now play through the notes of the scale in descending order.

TRACK 09

Next, ascend and descend the scale continuously and apply alternate picking as indicated by the symbols above the tab.

Now let's apply a few of the scale patterns from the previous chapter. For the first example, apply the alternate-picking exercise by playing each note of the scale twice, as shown below.

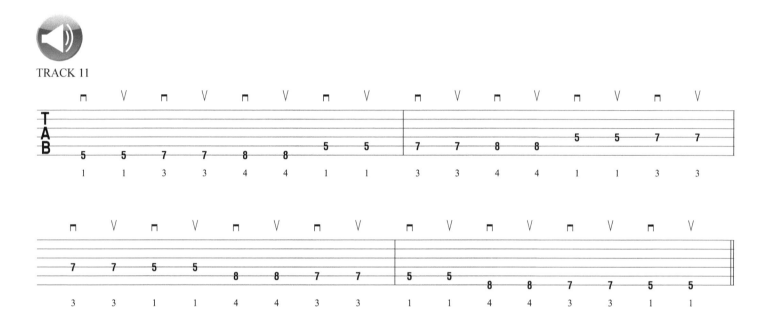

For this next example, ascend and descend the scale in groups of three.

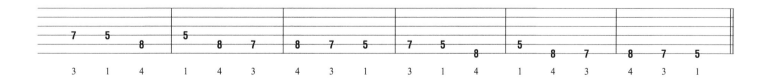

The previous version of the A minor scale, which starts at the fifth fret, is known as a *closed-position* scale because it contains no open strings. You can also start the scale on the fifth string by moving your hand to first position (first finger at the first fret) and utilizing the open strings to play the scale as an *open-position* scale. When playing open position scales, take care so as not to let the notes ring out over each other, especially when descending the scale.

In the scale diagram below, there are some white and black dots with no finger numbers to the left of the diagram. These indicate the open strings in the scale. As before, white dots represent the root notes, A, and the black dots represent the other notes of the scale. The tab staff below the diagram shows the scale both ascending and descending. The "0" tab numbers with no finger numbers beneath them indicate the open strings.

A Minor Scale (open-position)

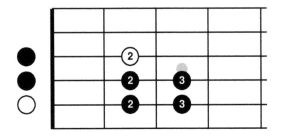

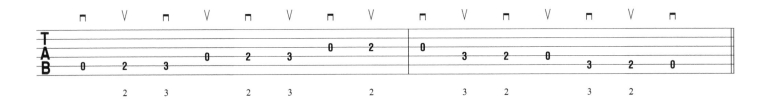

Now play the pattern from the previous page, using the open-position scale. Try to use steady alternate picking, and keep the open strings from ringing out over the other notes.

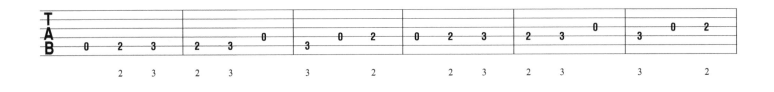

Chapter 4
Scale Theory and Transposing

Although you don't need to read traditional music to play the scales and examples in this book, it helps to know a little bit about the music theory behind them. This will help you to learn the notes on the guitar and play scales in any key.

Intervals of the Musical Alphabet

An *interval* is the distance in pitch (highness or lowness) between two notes. The natural notes of the musical alphabet (A–B–C–D–E–F–G) are separated by two different types of intervals—*half steps* and *whole steps*. On any single guitar string, the distance of one fret in either direction is a half step; the distance of two frets in either direction is a whole step.

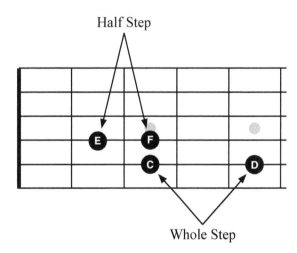

In the musical alphabet, natural half steps occur between the notes B and C, and E and F. All of the other natural notes are separated by natural whole steps.

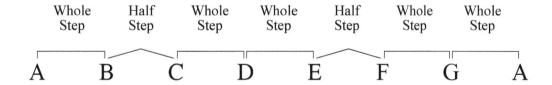

Notice that the above series of notes and intervals makes up the A natural minor scale. This information gives us the interval formula (W–H–W–W–H–W–W) for the minor scale. All natural minor scales, no matter the key, contain this same series of half steps and whole steps. An easy way to memorize this minor scale formula is to remember that the half steps occur between the second and third steps of the scale, and between the fifth and sixth steps of the scale; all of the other intervals are whole steps.

Let's take another look at the C major scale and see where the half steps and whole steps occur.

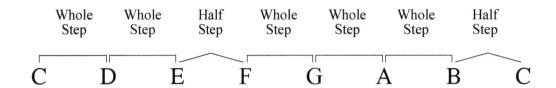

Whole Step	Whole Step	Half Step	Whole Step	Whole Step	Whole Step	Half Step

C   D   E   F   G   A   B   C

This information gives us the interval formula (W–W–H–W–W–W–H) for the major scale. All major scales, no matter the key, contain this same series of half steps and whole steps. The half steps occur between the third and fourth steps of the scale, and between the seventh and eighth (octave) steps of the scale. All of the other intervals are whole steps.

Let's transpose the major scale to another key. Because of the way the guitar is tuned, the same major and minor scale patterns you've already learned can be started at any note on the fifth or sixth strings. If we take the C major scale pattern and move it so that it starts on the note G at the third fret of the sixth string, this will give us a G major scale.

G Major Scale

TRACK 13

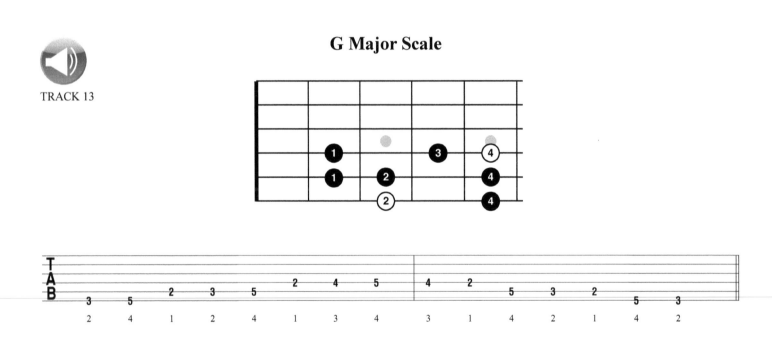

Here are the notes of the G major scale, using the same whole step/half step formula from above. If we take the letter names of the musical alphabet from G to G, we need to manipulate the interval between the seventh and eighth steps by raising the F a half step to F♯, giving us the correct order of half steps and whole steps.

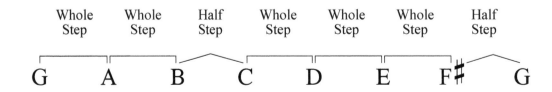

Whole Step	Whole Step	Half Step	Whole Step	Whole Step	Whole Step	Half Step

G   A   B   C   D   E   F♯   G

Let's transpose the scale again. We can move the C major scale pattern up the fretboard so that it starts on the note F at the eighth fret of the fifth string. This will give us the F major scale.

F Major Scale

TRACK 14

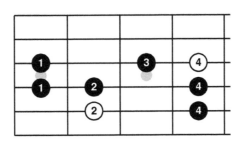

7 fr.

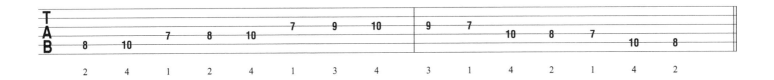

Here are the notes of the F major scale. If we take the letter names of the musical alphabet from F to F, we need to manipulate the interval between the third and fourth steps by lowering the B a half step to B♭, giving us the correct order of half steps and whole steps.

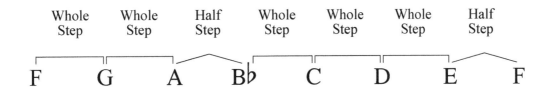

Whole Step	Whole Step	Half Step	Whole Step	Whole Step	Whole Step	Half Step
F	G	A	B♭	C	D	E	F

Now let's transpose the closed-position A natural minor scale up two frets and start it on the note B at the seventh fret of the sixth string. This will give us a B natural minor scale (the tab is presented at the top of the next page).

B Minor Scale

TRACK 15

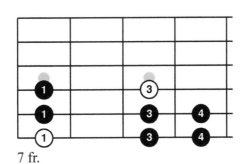

7 fr.

Here are the notes of the B minor scale showing the whole step/half step formula. If we take the letter names of the musical alphabet from B to B, we need to add sharps to C and F, which will give us the correct series of intervals.

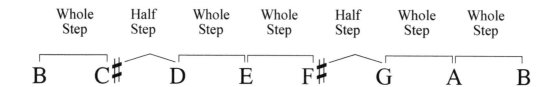

Let's try another minor key. By moving the closed-position A minor scale up one string and starting at the fifth fret of the fifth string, we get the D minor scale.

D Minor Scale

TRACK 16

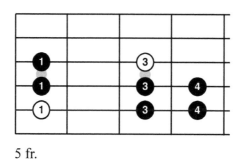

5 fr.

Here are the notes of the D minor scale showing the whole step/half step formula. If we take the letter names of the musical alphabet from D to D, we need to change the B to B♭, which will give us the correct series of intervals.

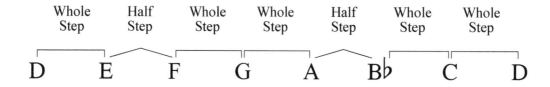

In order to transpose the scales to any key, it's helpful to learn and memorize the notes on the fretboard. You can use your knowledge of the musical alphabet to determine where all of the natural notes are located. You should already know the names of the open strings: E–A–D–G–B–E. From there, use the whole step/half step formula of the musical alphabet to find the other notes. Below are the regular letter-name notes on the sixth string (E), with the half steps and whole steps indicated.

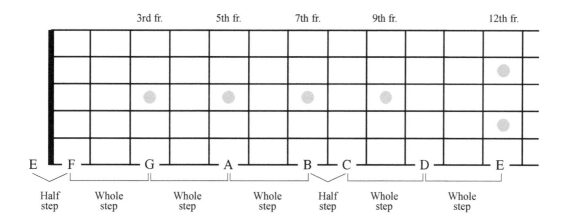

The notes that fall in-between the natural whole steps are sharps or flats. A sharp placed on a note raises its pitch by a half step; a flat placed on a note lowers its pitch by a half step. For example, the note between A and B can be called either A♯ or B♭ (depending on the key and context of the music). Below is a diagram that shows all of the notes on the sixth string, including the sharp and flat notes, from the low open E to the next, higher E at the 12th fret. After the 12th fret, the musical alphabet repeats (the note at the 13th fret is F, the note at the 14th fret is F♯, and so on).

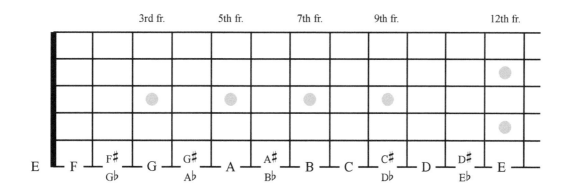

Here's a diagram that shows all of the notes on the fifth string. Memorizing the notes on the fifth and sixth strings are essential for guitarists, but you can repeat this process for the other four strings, as well.

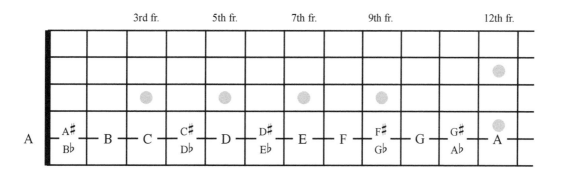

17

Rhythm Notation

Along with melody and harmony, rhythm is one of the most important elements of music. Although it isn't essential for you to learn how to read musical notes at this point, it is helpful to learn how to count rhythms and play in time. Rhythmic notation can be shown in tablature by using the same system of stems and beams that are used in traditional music notation. Many of the scale patterns and exercises in this book should be played in strict time to maximize your potential and yield the most benefit to your playing technique. In this section, we'll go through the basic rhythm notation you should know in order to count out and perform the exercises in this book.

In 4/4 time (common time), a *quarter note* is equal to one beat, and four quarter notes make up a complete measure of music.

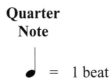

In tablature, numbers on the staff are used instead of noteheads. The traditional stems, flags, and beams are attached to the tab numbers to depict rhythmic notation. Below is the C major scale played in quarter notes (a single stem is attached to each number to represent one beat for each note). The rhythmic count is shown above the tab staff. Count "one, two, three, four" for each measure, playing one note of the scale for each beat. Don't pause or hesitate between notes, and be sure to keep the rhythm steady.

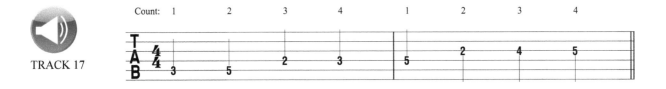

TRACK 17

Whole notes are held for four beats, and *half notes* are held for two beats. Both are indicated by using open circles for noteheads (shown below). In tablature, whole notes and half notes are distinguished by adding circles around the tab numbers.

The next example uses a combination of quarter notes, half notes, and whole notes to play some of the notes of the G minor scale, beginning at the third fret of the sixth string. This is a rhythm exercise designed to help you become familiar with the note values. Follow the count above the tab staff and play at a smooth, even tempo. Remember to keep proper technique in your fretting hand and apply alternate picking throughout.

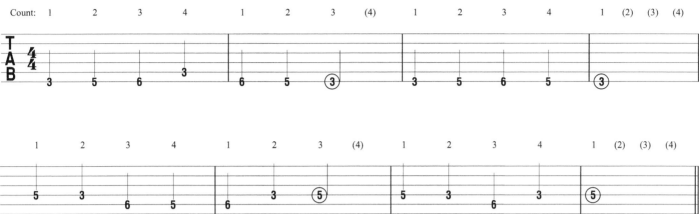

Eighth notes are held for half of a beat. A single eighth note is notated by using a single flag on its stem (shown below). Multiple eighth notes are usually joined at the top with a horizontal beam instead of flags.

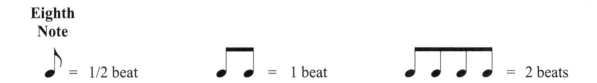

Eighth notes can be counted using "and" in-between the beats ("one-and, two-and," etc.). The example below uses steady eighth notes to ascend and descend the D major scale in groups of four.

TRACK 19

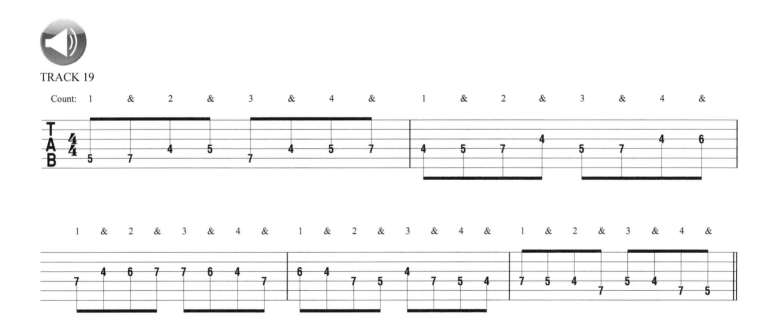

Sixteenth notes are held for one quarter of a beat. A single 16th note is notated using a double flag on its stem. Multiple 16th notes that all fall within the same beat can be grouped together using a double horizontal beam instead of flags. The example below is an alternate-picking exercise using the B minor scale, starting at the second fret of the fifth string. For 16th notes, count "one-e-and-a, two-e-and-a," etc.

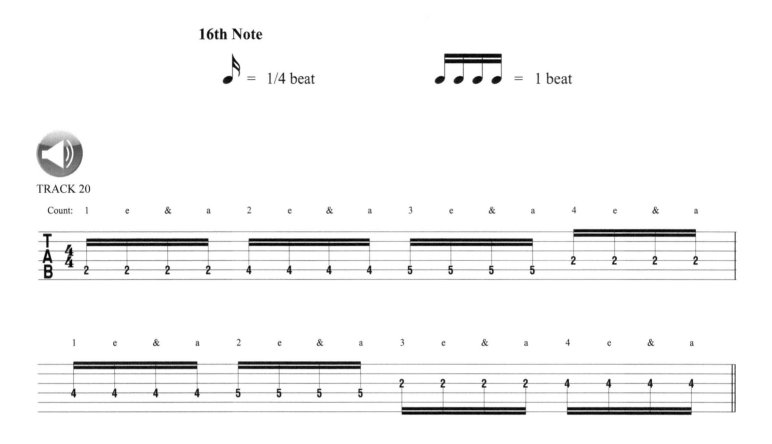

Rests

A rest is used to indicate silence—where no note or chord is played. Rests also have rhythmic values that tell you how long the silence should last. The universal symbols for musical rests are shown below; these same symbols are also used in tablature.

Whole Rest (4 beats)	Half Rest (2 beats)	Quarter Rest (1 beat)	Eighth Rest (1/2 beat)	16th Rest (1/4 beat)

Triplets

A triplet is a group of three equivalent notes played within the space of two. The most common triplet is the eighth-note triplet, wherein three notes are played within one beat, dividing the beat into three equal-length notes. Eighth-note triplets are counted "one-and-a, two-and-a," etc. Triplets are indicated by using a "3" above the beamed or bracketed group of notes. The following example plays through the F minor scale in groups of three using a triplet rhythm.

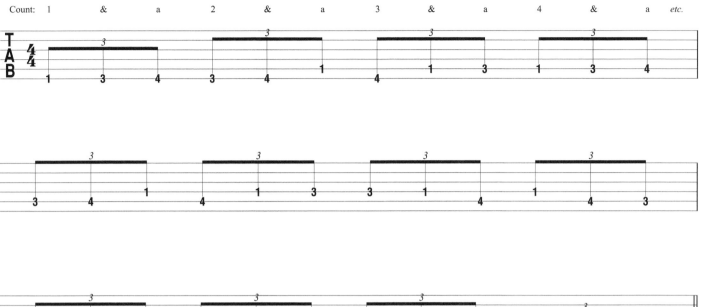

Review

The following chart summarizes some of the various rhythm values and rest symbols used throughout this book.

NAME OF NOTE	RHYTHM NOTATION	REST SYMBOLS	COUNTS (AND NUMBER OF BEATS)
Whole Note	𝅝	𝄻	𝅝 1 (2) (3) (4)
Half Note	𝅗𝅥	𝄼	𝅗𝅥 𝅗𝅥 1 (2) 3 (4)
Quarter Note	𝅘𝅥	𝄽	𝅘𝅥 𝅘𝅥 𝅘𝅥 𝅘𝅥 1 2 3 4
Eighth Note	𝅘𝅥𝅮 𝅘𝅥𝅮𝅘𝅥𝅮	𝄾	𝅘𝅥𝅮𝅘𝅥𝅮 𝅘𝅥𝅮𝅘𝅥𝅮 𝅘𝅥𝅮𝅘𝅥𝅮 𝅘𝅥𝅮𝅘𝅥𝅮 1 & 2 & 3 & 4 &
16th Note	𝅘𝅥𝅯 𝅘𝅥𝅯𝅘𝅥𝅯	𝄿	𝅘𝅥𝅯𝅘𝅥𝅯𝅘𝅥𝅯𝅘𝅥𝅯 𝅘𝅥𝅯𝅘𝅥𝅯𝅘𝅥𝅯𝅘𝅥𝅯 𝅘𝅥𝅯𝅘𝅥𝅯𝅘𝅥𝅯𝅘𝅥𝅯 𝅘𝅥𝅯𝅘𝅥𝅯𝅘𝅥𝅯𝅘𝅥𝅯 1 e & a 2 e & a 3 e & a 4 e & a
Eighth-Note Triplet	$\overset{3}{\overline{}}$ 𝅘𝅥𝅮𝅘𝅥𝅮𝅘𝅥𝅮		𝅘𝅥𝅮𝅘𝅥𝅮𝅘𝅥𝅮 𝅘𝅥𝅮𝅘𝅥𝅮𝅘𝅥𝅮 𝅘𝅥𝅮𝅘𝅥𝅮𝅘𝅥𝅮 𝅘𝅥𝅮𝅘𝅥𝅮𝅘𝅥𝅮 1 & a 2 & a 3 & a 4 & a

Chapter 5
Scale Patterns and Alternate Fingerings

Let's begin this section with a series of scale patterns using various rhythms. We'll start by using the fingerings for the one-octave major and minor scales from previous chapters, then we'll apply some alternate fingerings to expand your scale vocabulary.

For this first pattern, we'll use a combination of eighth and quarter notes to ascend the G major scale in sections, then we'll reverse the pattern and descend the scale.

TRACK 22

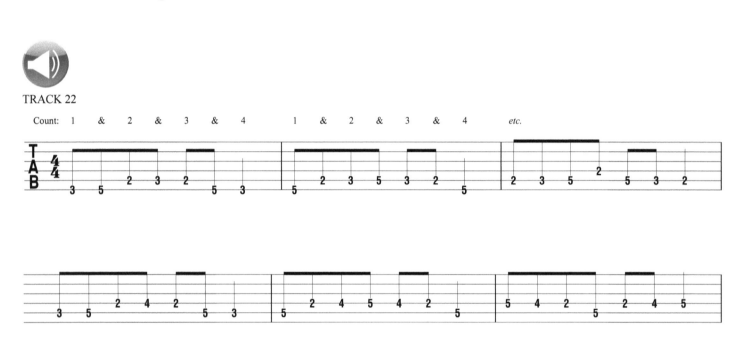

Let's try a similar pattern with a combination of triplets and half notes for the rhythm, this time using the C minor scale.

TRACK 23

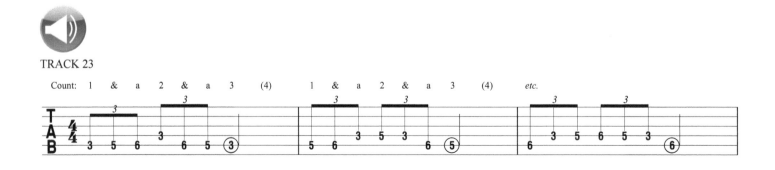

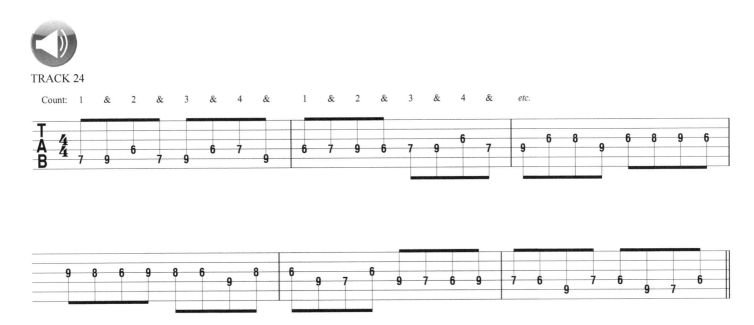

Here's an eighth-note pattern using the E major scale, beginning at the seventh fret of the fifth string.

TRACK 24

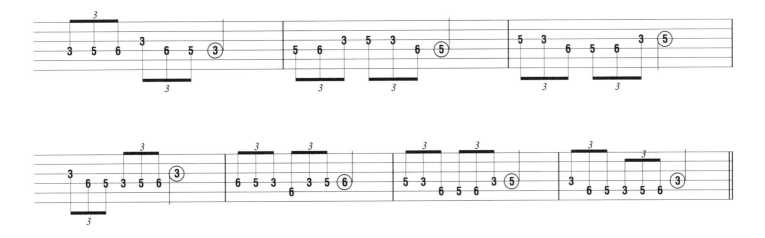

For this next exercise, ascend and descend the G major scale in intervals of 3rds as shown below, then move the entire pattern up one half step (one fret) and play it in the key of A♭ major. Continue chromatically (one fret at a time) up the fretboard.

TRACK 25

Alternate Scale Fingerings

In addition to the scale fingerings from the previous chapters, there are a few other useful fingerings for the one-octave major and minor scales. The following alternate fingering for the A minor scale starts with your fourth finger at the fifth fret of the sixth string.

A Minor Scale

TRACK 26

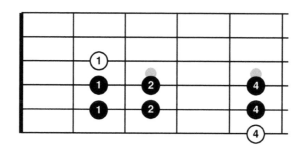

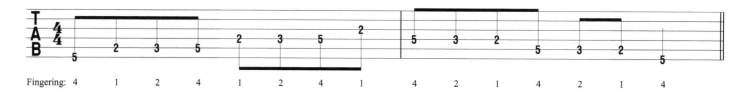

Fingering: 4   1   2   4   1   2   4   1   4   2   1   4   2   1   4

If we move the above minor scale pattern up a string so that it starts on the fifth string, the scale fingering will be slightly different. This is to compensate for the guitar's tuning—the interval between the second and third strings is a 3rd, while the intervals between all of the other strings is a 4th. Here's the D minor scale starting with your fourth finger at the fifth fret of the fifth string.

D Minor Scale

TRACK 27

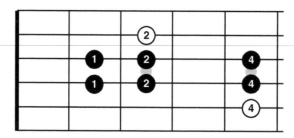

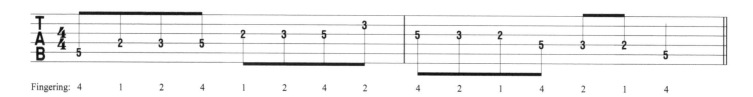

Fingering: 4   1   2   4   1   2   4   2   4   2   1   4   2   1   4

Once you have the above scale fingerings memorized, apply the previous scale patterns to them and practice transposing and playing the scales in different areas of the fretboard.

Because of the guitar's tuning, the one-octave major scale can be easily played when starting with your fourth finger on the fifth string. Here's an E major scale starting at the seventh fret of the fifth string.

E Major Scale

TRACK 28

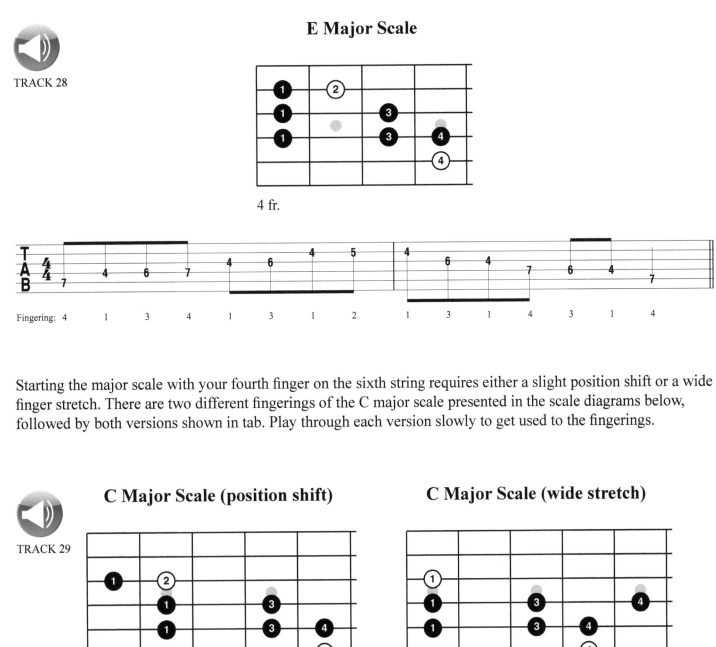

4 fr.

Fingering: 4   1   3   4   1   3   1   2   1   3   1   4   3   1   4

Starting the major scale with your fourth finger on the sixth string requires either a slight position shift or a wide finger stretch. There are two different fingerings of the C major scale presented in the scale diagrams below, followed by both versions shown in tab. Play through each version slowly to get used to the fingerings.

C Major Scale (position shift)   ## C Major Scale (wide stretch)

TRACK 29

4 fr.   5 fr.

(position shift)

Fingering: 4   1   3   4   1   3   1   2   1   3   1   4   3   1   4

(wide stretch)

Fingering: 4   1   3   4   1   3   4   1   4   3   1   4   3   1   4

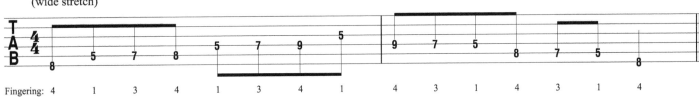
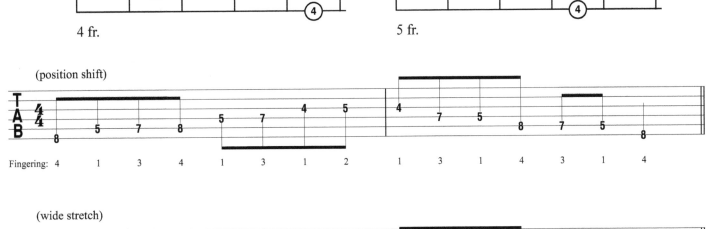

The following alternate fingerings for the major and minor scales require some wide stretches. They can be played by starting on either the fifth or sixth string without altering the pattern.

Here's a different fingering for the B minor scale, starting with your second finger at the seventh fret of the sixth string. Follow the tab and fingering closely and practice slowly at first to get used to the wide spacing between the fretted notes.

B Minor Scale

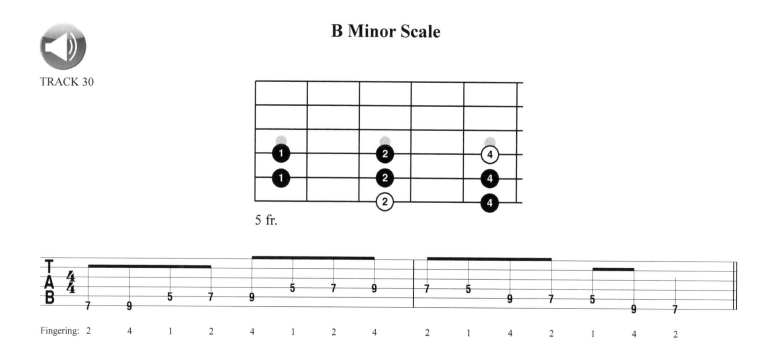

TRACK 30

5 fr.

This version of the F major scale begins with your first finger at the first fret of the sixth string. This scale fingering is a bit of a challenge, but if you can play it in the first position as shown below, it will be easy to move it up the fretboard and play it in different keys. Remember: you can also play this same scale pattern by starting on any note on the fifth string.

F Major Scale

TRACK 31

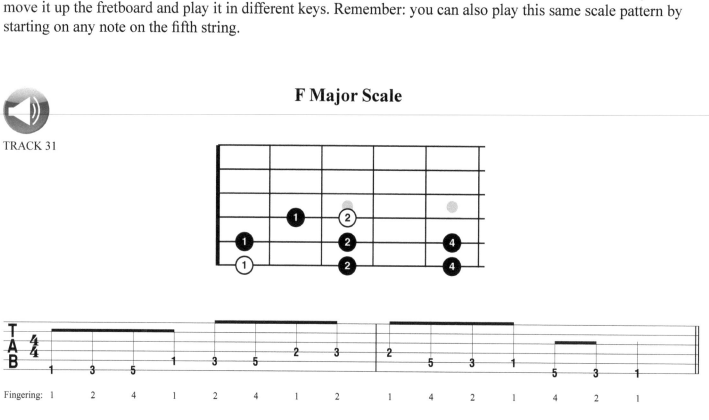

Here's a challenging scale pattern that uses the minor scale fingering from the previous page. It begins with the G minor scale, starting at the third fret of the sixth string with your second finger. From there, it ascends the scale in groups of three using an eighth-note rhythm. Once you get to the octave, move the scale pattern up one fret to A♭ minor and descend in groups of three. Continue in this fashion (chromatically) up the fretboard. Between the rhythm and the wide finger stretches, this one will be difficult at first. Once you've got it down, it will be useful as a great warm-up exercise. Start slowly and build speed gradually.

TRACK 32

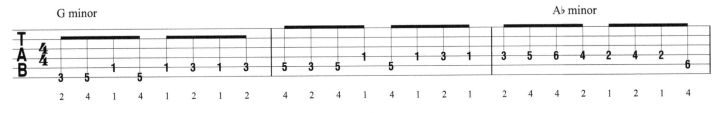

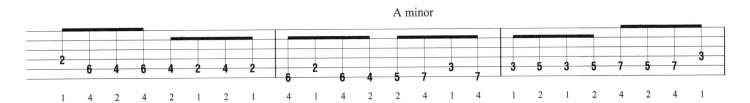

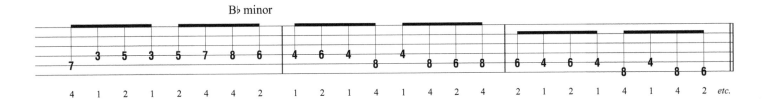

Here's another exercise using the major scale fingering from the previous page. Start with the F major scale at the first fret of the sixth string, using your first finger. Ascend the scale in intervals of 3rds, and when you reach the octave, move up one fret and descend the F♯ major scale in 3rds. Continue chromatically up the fretboard as we did in the exercise above.

TRACK 33

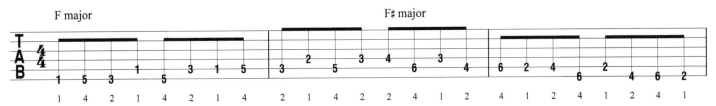

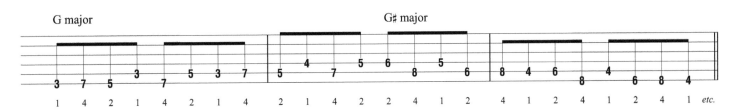

Two-Octave Scales

Let's extend the scales to include the higher strings on the guitar. If we start the major or minor scale on the sixth string, we can play a full two octaves of the scale without changing positions on the fretboard. Here's a two-octave A major scale, starting with your second finger at the fifth fret of the sixth string. Memorize the fingering and the placement of the root notes.

TRACK 34

Two-Octave A Major Scale

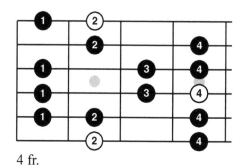

4 fr.

Fingering: 2 4 1 2 4 1 3 4 1 3 4 2 4 1 2

Here's a scale pattern exercise using the above two-octave major scale. Ascend the scale in groups of four notes until you reach the highest note, then reverse the pattern and descend the scale from the highest note to the lowest note.

TRACK 35

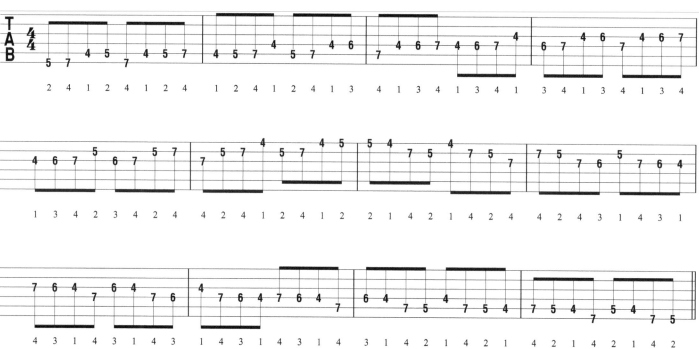

28

Here's a two-octave B minor scale, starting with your first finger at the seventh fret of the sixth string. Follow the fingering closely and take note of the slight backwards shift to the sixth fret that occurs on the third string.

Two-Octave B Minor Scale

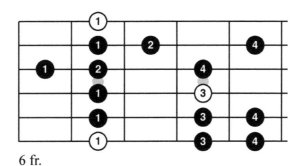

6 fr.

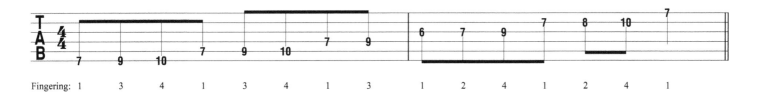

Fingering: 1   3   4   1   3   4   1   3   1   2   4   1   2   4   1

Here's the same scale pattern exercise that we used for the major scale on the previous page, this time applied to the two-octave B minor scale. Notice the suggested fingering adjustments for the slight position shifts that occur on the third string. Depending on the context of a pattern, riff, or solo, you'll find that applying slight variations to the scale fingerings will make transitions smoother and easier.

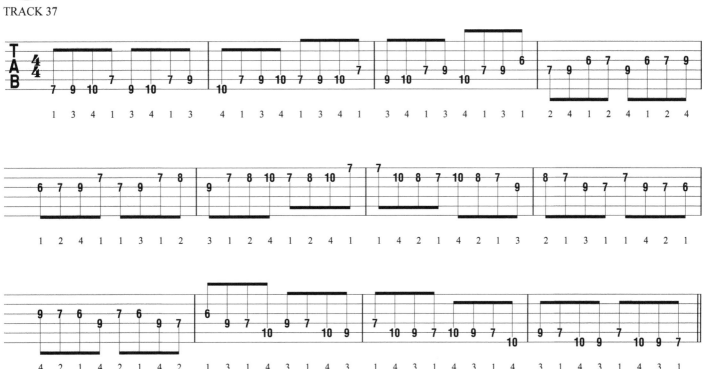

29

Chapter 6
Pentatonic Scales

Pentatonic scales are five-note scales that are abbreviated versions of the regular seven-note major and minor scales. Pentatonic scales are the most commonly used scales for riffs and solos in popular music, so it's essential that you master them.

The Major Pentatonic Scale

Here's one octave of the G major pentatonic scale, starting with your second finger at the third fret of the sixth string. Notice how much easier this scale is to play than the regular major scale; there are only two notes per string.

TRACK 38

G Major Pentatonic Scale

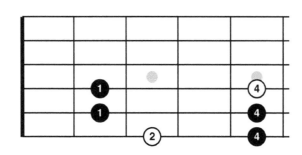

The chart below compares the G major scale and the G major pentatonic scale. By omitting the fourth and seventh steps of the major scale, we get the notes of the major pentatonic scale.

	root	2nd	3rd	4th	5th	6th	7th	octave
G Major	G	A	B	C	D	E	F♯	G

	root	2nd	3rd		5th	6th		octave
G Major Pentatonic	G	A	B		D	E		G

There are five distinct scale patterns (positions) of the major pentatonic scale, each beginning on a different note of the scale. The first position starts with the first (root) note of the scale, the second position begins on the second note of the scale, and so on. By learning all five positions, you'll be able to play the notes of the major pentatonic scale anywhere on the fretboard. If you keep track of where the root notes are located in each position, you'll be able to transpose the scale positions to any key.

G Major Pentatonic Scale: 1st Position

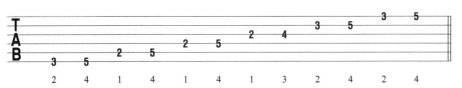

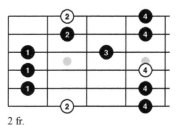

G Major Pentatonic Scale: 2nd Position

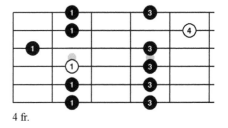

G Major Pentatonic Scale: 3rd Position

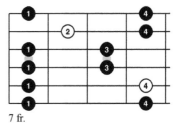

G Major Pentatonic Scale: 4th Position

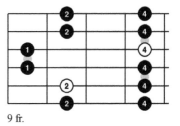

G Major Pentatonic Scale: 5th Position

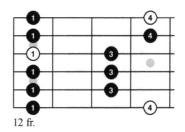

The following exercise uses a triplet rhythm to ascend and descend each of the scale positions in groups of three notes. Start with the first position scale, ascending in triplets until you get to the highest note in that position, then move up to the next scale position and descend it by using the pattern in reverse. Continue through the rest of the scale positions in this fashion until you reach the top of the fifth position.

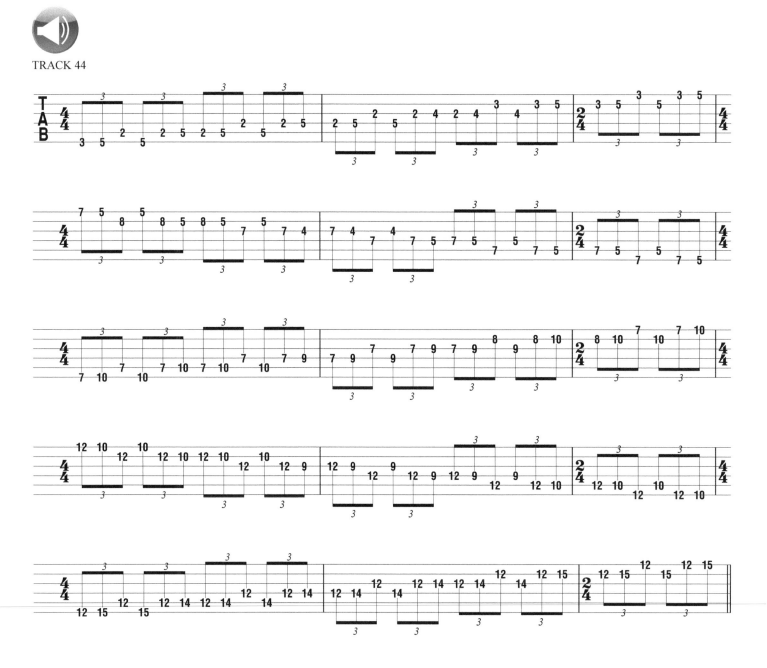

To give you a better sense of how the scale patterns overlap and span the entire fretboard, here's a complete fretboard diagram of the G major pentatonic scale with the positions indicated by brackets. All of the root notes (G) are indicated with white circles; all of the other notes are indicated with black circles.

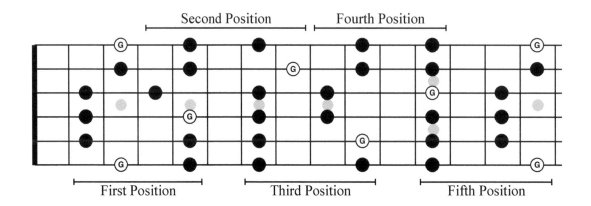

The Minor Pentatonic Scale

The minor pentatonic scale is the most popular scale for rock riffs and solos. Here's one octave of the A minor pentatonic scale, starting with your first finger at the fifth fret of the sixth string.

A Minor Pentatonic Scale

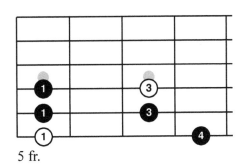

5 fr.

The chart below compares the A minor scale and the A minor pentatonic scale. By omitting the second and sixth steps of the minor scale, we get the notes of the minor pentatonic scale.

	root	2nd	♭3rd	4th	5th	♭6th	♭7th	octave
A Minor	A	B	C	D	E	F	G	A

	root		♭3rd	4th	5th		♭7th	octave
A Minor Pentatonic	A		C	D	E		G	A

Here are the five scale positions for the A minor pentatonic scale, starting with the first position at the fifth fret on the sixth string. The fifth position scale on the following page has been transposed one octave lower and starts at the third fret. Memorize where the root notes are so you can transpose the scale positions to any key.

A Minor Pentatonic Scale: 1st Position

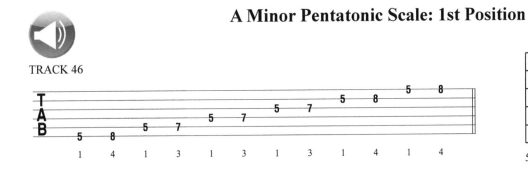

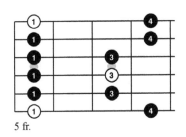

5 fr.

33

A Minor Pentatonic Scale: 2nd Position

TRACK 47

TRACK 47

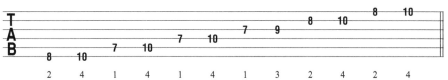

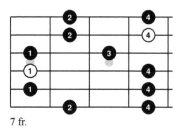

7 fr.

A Minor Pentatonic Scale: 3rd Position

TRACK 48

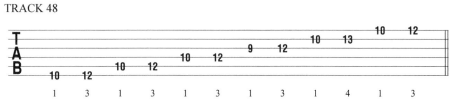

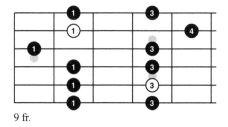

9 fr.

A Minor Pentatonic Scale: 4th Position

TRACK 49

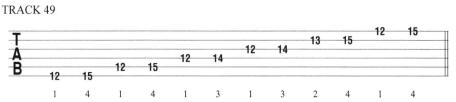

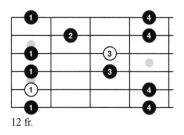

12 fr.

A Minor Pentatonic Scale: 5th Position

TRACK 50

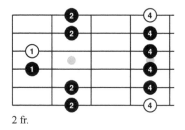

2 fr.

The following exercise utilizes the A minor pentatonic scale. Start by playing the first four notes of the scale, then descend the scale to the starting note. Continue up the scale in groups of four notes until you reach the top of the position, then play the pattern in reverse and descend the scale in groups of four. The pattern is shown here using the first-position scale; once you've got it down, apply the pattern to the other four scale positions.

TRACK 51

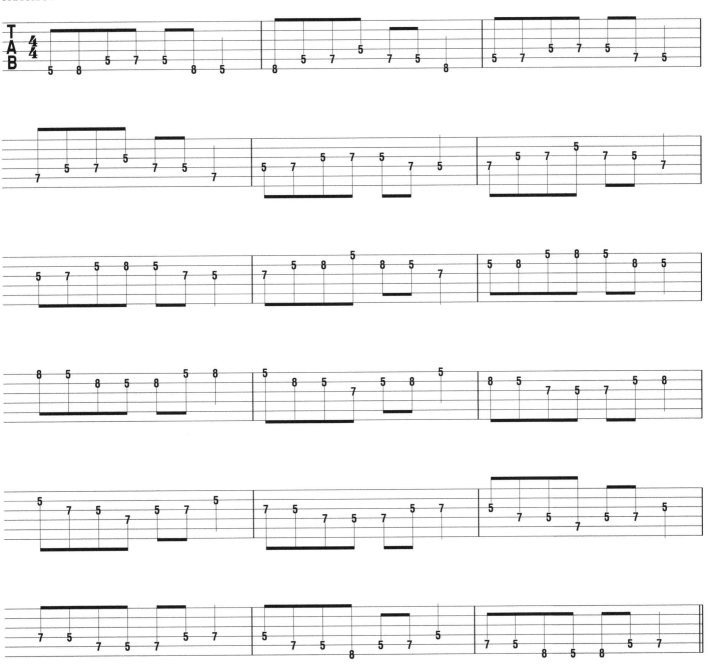

Here's a complete fretboard diagram of the A minor pentatonic scale with the positions indicated by brackets. All of the root notes (A) are indicated with white circles; all of the other notes are indicated with black circles.

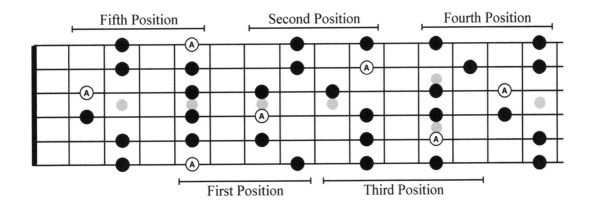

Chapter 7
Blues Scales

The blues scale is a slight variation of the minor pentatonic scale that includes one extra note between the fourth and fifth steps of the scale. This particular note is the ♭5th of the scale, also known as the *blues tritone*. Here's one octave of the A blues scale, starting with your first finger at the fifth fret of the sixth string.

TRACK 52

A Blues Scale

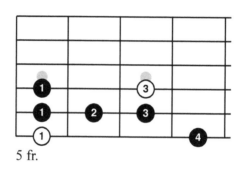

5 fr.

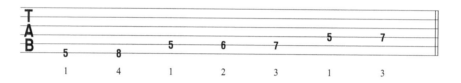

Here are the five positions of the A blues scale. The only difference between these diagrams and the minor pentatonic scale positions from the previous chapter is the addition of the blues tritone. Notice that some of the fingerings have been adjusted to compensate for the additional notes.

1st Position

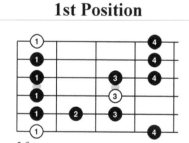

5 fr.

2nd Position

7 fr.

3rd Position

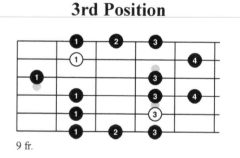

9 fr.

4th Position

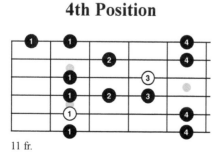

11 fr.

5th Position

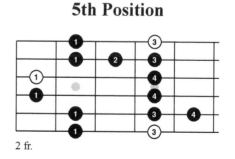

2 fr.

You can also add a chromatic passing tone to the major pentatonic scale (this time, between the second and third steps) to create a major version of the blues scale. Here's one octave of the G major blues scale.

G Major Blues Scale

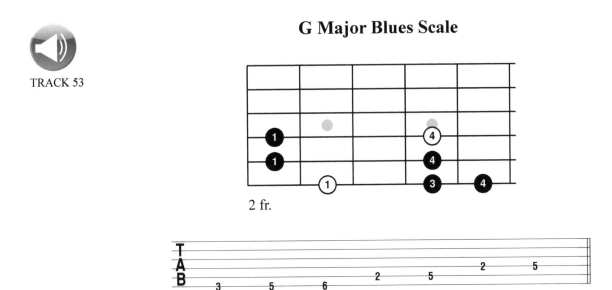

TRACK 53

2 fr.

The blues scales are widely used on the guitar to play riffs in open-position keys. The scales are somewhat easier to play in open position and sound great. Here's an open-position E major blues scale shown in tab, starting with the low open E on the sixth string.

Open E Major Blues Scale

TRACK 54

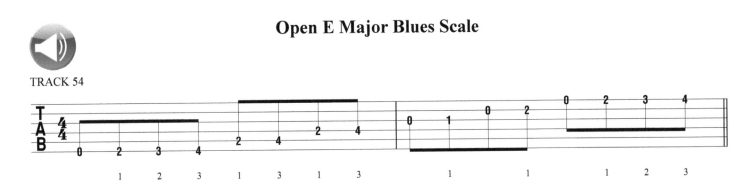

Another popular key to play in open position is A minor. Blues scales are generally assumed to be based on the minor pentatonic scale. This is why we simply call this scale the "A blues scale," and use the word "major" when referring to the major version above.

Open A Blues Scale

TRACK 55

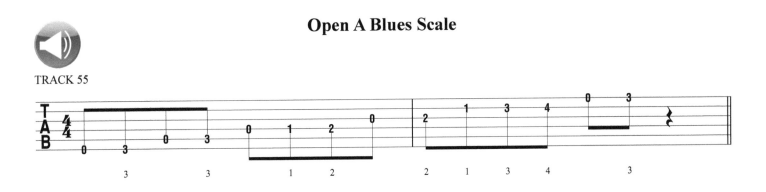

Chapter 8
The Five Positions of the Major and Minor Scales

As with the pentatonic scales, we can play all of the notes of the major or minor scales anywhere on the fretboard by using five distinct scale positions. In this chapter, we'll explore all five positions, learn where the root notes are located, and apply some scale pattern exercises to help you practice and memorize the positions.

The Five Positions of the G Major Scale

Here are the five scale positions in the key of G major. Each position of the scale contains every note in the key of G major that is comfortably within reach. The first position begins at the second fret of the sixth string.

G Major Scale: 1st Position

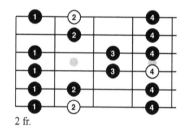

G Major Scale: 2nd Position

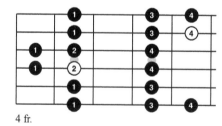

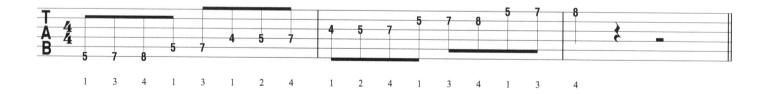

G Major Scale: 3rd Position

TRACK 58

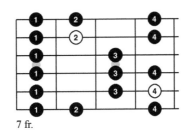

7 fr.

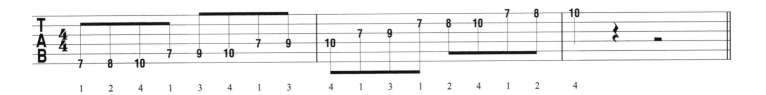

G Major Scale: 4th Position

TRACK 59

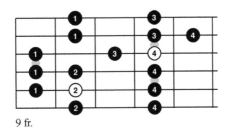

9 fr.

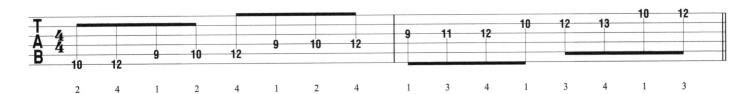

G Major Scale: 5th Position

TRACK 60

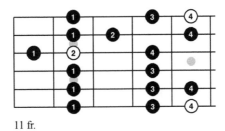

11 fr.

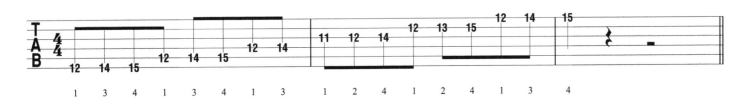

Here's an eighth-note scale pattern using the first-position G major scale. Once you've got the pattern down, apply it to the other four positions.

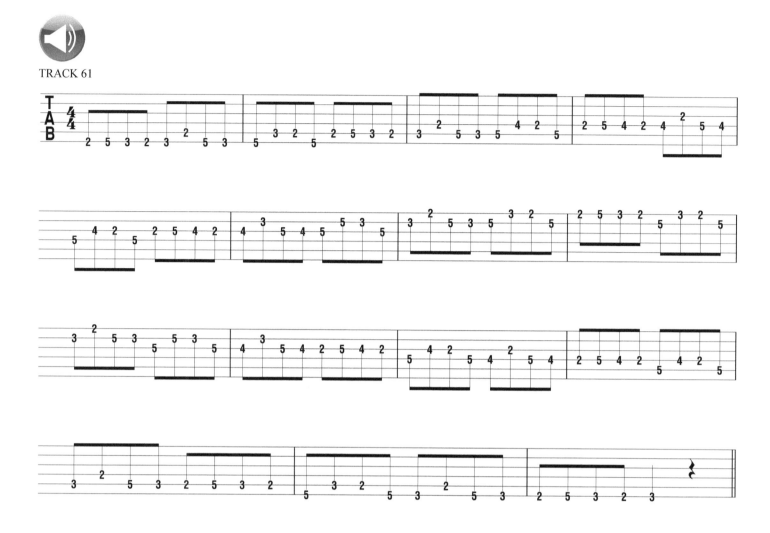

TRACK 61

The Five Positions of the A Minor Scale

Here are the five scale positions in the key of A minor, starting with the first-position scale at the fifth fret of the sixth string. The fifth-position scale has been moved down an octave and starts at the third fret.

A Minor Scale: 1st Position

TRACK 62

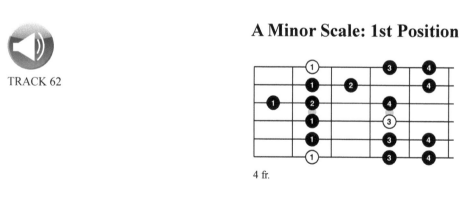

4 fr.

A Minor Scale: 2nd Position

TRACK 63

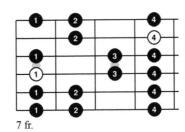

7 fr.

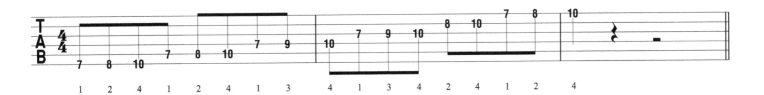

A Minor Scale: 3rd Position

TRACK 64

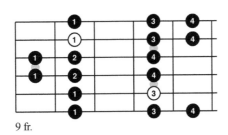

9 fr.

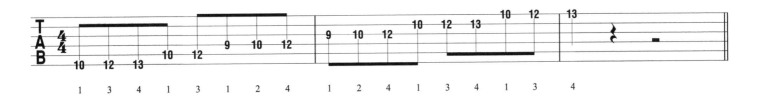

A Minor Scale: 4th Position

TRACK 65

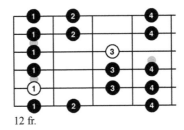

12 fr.

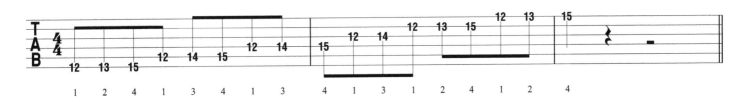

A Minor Scale: 5th Position

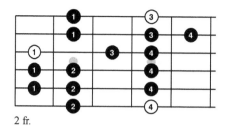

2 fr.

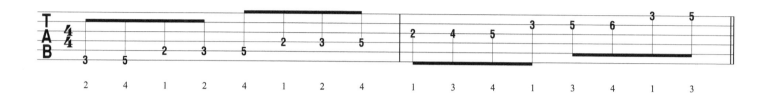

Here's a variation of the previous scale pattern, using the first-position A minor scale. Apply the pattern to the other four positions once you've got it.

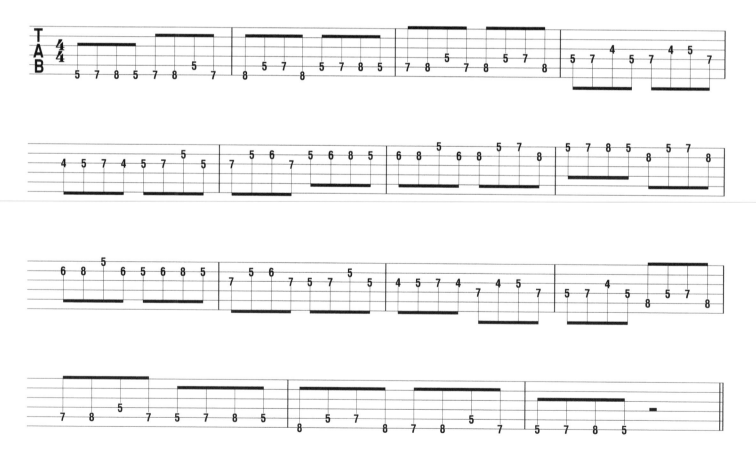

Chapter 9
Three-Octave Scales

The purpose of learning the five different scale positions is to get you to visualize a scale across the entire fretboard; however, most proficient players won't stay in one position for an entire solo. Learning to move seamlessly from position to position will allow you to play more interesting solos across a wider range. This chapter presents a few examples and suggested fingerings for playing the scales across three full octaves.

Three-Octave G Major Scale

Let's explore three different ways to play the three-octave G major scale. This first example might be the most comfortable version. As a suggestion, we've indicated that you should try to perform the ascending and descending slides with your first finger, but you're welcome to experiment and see what works best for you. The slides are indicated by arrows on the scale diagram, and by diagonal lines in the tab. One way to help you remember the pattern is to memorize the number of notes per string. Ascending, the amount of notes per string is: 4–4–3–4–3–4.

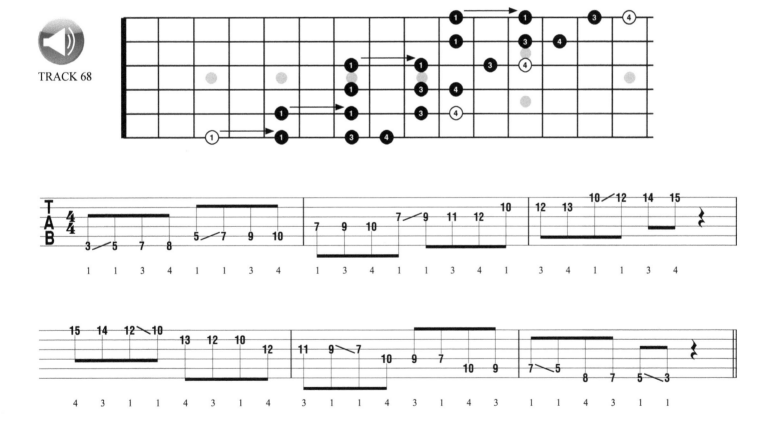

TRACK 68

The next version of the three-octave scale incorporates wide stretches using the first, second, and fourth fingers. Initially, this may seem more difficult compared to the previous example, but once you're comfortable with the finger span, you can attain great speed and accuracy with this technique, especially when employing quick hammer-ons and pull-offs. The number of notes per string in this variation is: 3–4–3–4–4–4.

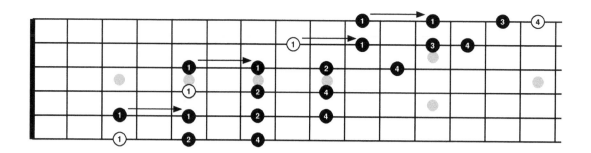

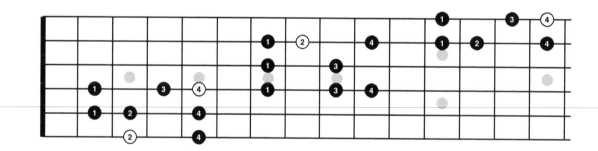

Here's a third way to play the three-octave scale, this time without slides. By shifting between larger portions of the scale positions in convenient places, you can split the fretboard up into three distinct sections. These sections are indicated by brackets above the tab staff. Notice that the fingering for the last part of the first section (1–3–4 on the fourth string) is the same as the fingering for the first part of the second section. This type of mirrored fingering happens again for the position shift on the second string (with a 1–2–4 fingering).

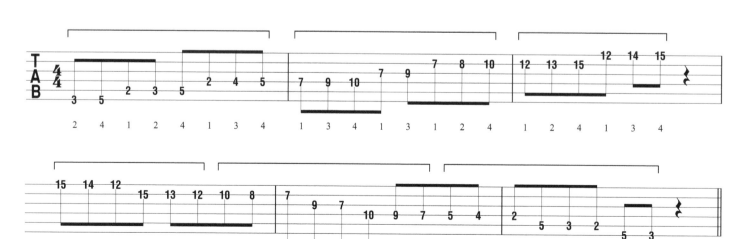

Three-Octave A Minor Scale

The first version of the following three-octave A minor scale uses ascending and descending fourth-finger slides. The 1–3–4 finger pattern is used consistently on strings 6–2.

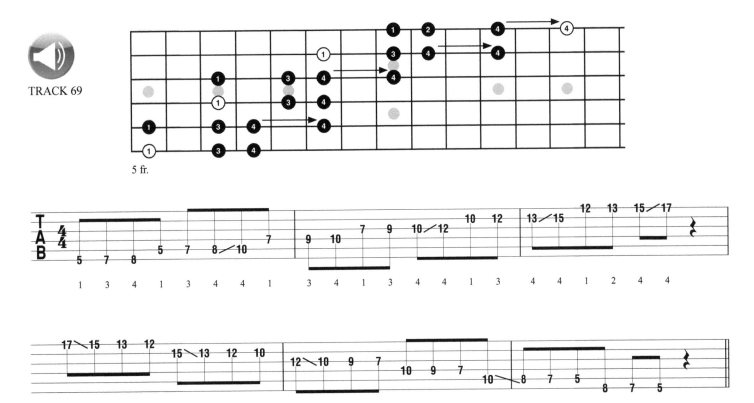

TRACK 69

This second version of the scale incorporates first-finger slides and wide 1–2–4 finger stretches.

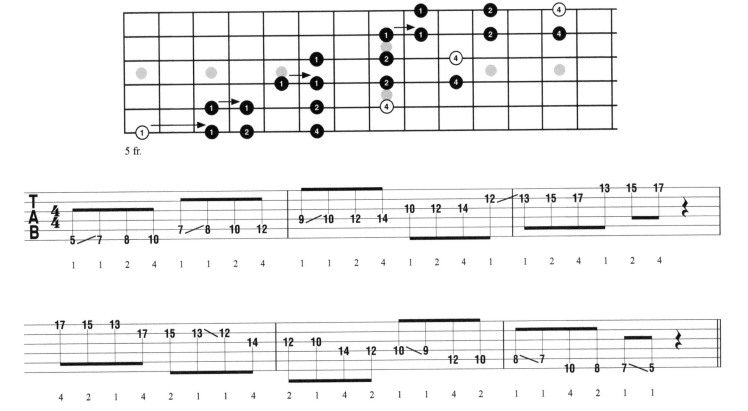

Now let's play the three-octave A minor scale in distinct sections, using the mirrored-fingering technique that we used for the G major scale. The 1–3–4 fingering is repeated on the sixth string to change positions, and then the 1–2–4 fingering is repeated on the fourth string to shift up to the 14th fret, where we finish off the rest of the scale.

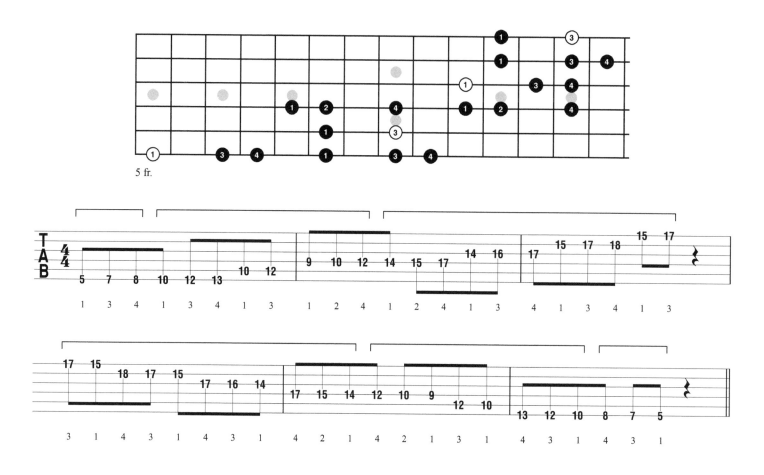

Three-Octave G Major Pentatonic Scale

As shown in the earlier chapter on pentatonic scales, we can subtract some of the notes from the G major scale to create the G major pentatonic. Here's a version of the three-octave G major pentatonic scale. Remember: there are multiple ways to connect the different scale positions; this is just one suggestion.

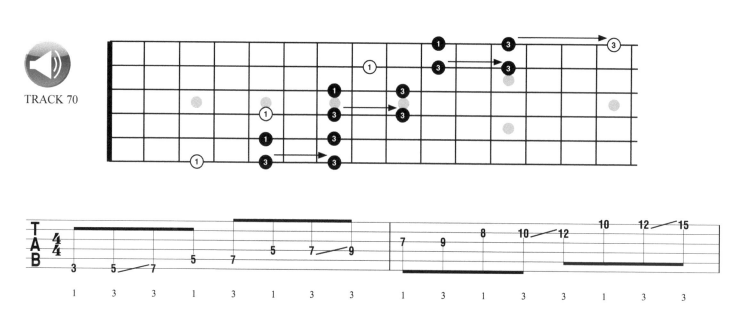

TRACK 70

Three-Octave A Minor Pentatonic Scale

Here's a suggested fingering for the three-octave A minor pentatonic scale. The slides on the sixth, fifth, and first strings are a little less comfortable since they use the fourth finger, but the rest of the scale pattern is easy. As with all of the scales in this book, practice transposing the pattern to other keys.

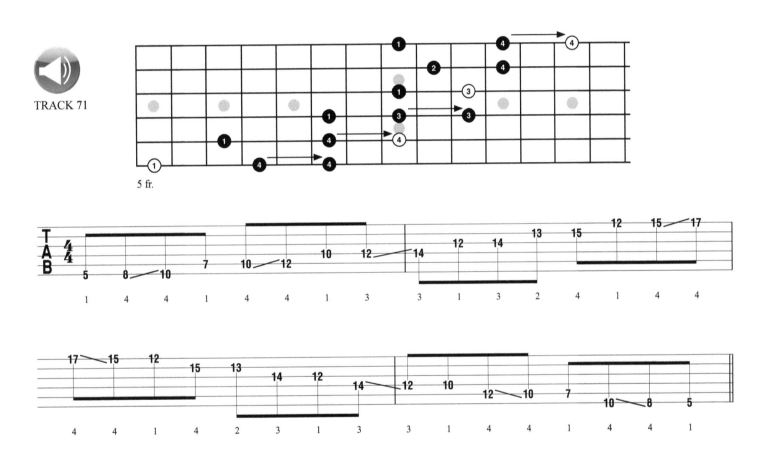

TRACK 71

Conclusion

The scales covered in this book represent the most popular scales for the modern guitarist. The major, minor, pentatonic, and blues scales are used extensively in all styles of popular music and they should give you the vocabulary you need for playing melodies, riffs, and solos. Practice transposing the scales to other popular keys, apply the scale pattern exercises to all of the scales, and use them to formulate your own unique practice and warm-up routines. Advanced guitarists will go on to study other scale variations and modes not covered in this book, but the scales you've learned here are a good place to start and represent a solid foundation for more advanced scales and techniques.

TEACH YOURSELF TO PLAY
GUITAR SONGS

Teach yourself to play your favorite songs on guitar with this multi-media learning experience! Each song in each book includes a comprehensive online video lesson with an interactive song transcription, slow-down features, looping capabilities, track choices, play-along functions, and more. The price of the books includes access to all of these online features!

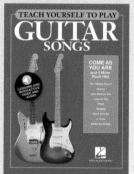

"COME AS YOU ARE" & 9 MORE ROCK HITS

Come As You Are (Nirvana) • Do I Wanna Know? (Artic Monkeys) • Heaven (Los Lonely Boys) • Here Without You (3 Doors Down) • Learn to Fly (Foo Fighters) • Plush (Stone Temple Pilots) • Santeria (Sublime) • Say It Ain't So (Weezer) • 21 Guns (Green Day) • Under the Bridge (Red Hot Chili Peppers).

Book with Online Audio & Video
00152224 .... $17.99

"MORE THAN WORDS" & 9 MORE ACOUSTIC HITS

Angie (The Rolling Stones) • Daughters (John Mayer) • Drive (Incubus) • Iris (Goo Goo Dolls) • Layla (Eric Clapton) • Mr. Jones (Counting Crows) • More Than Words (Extreme) • Patience (Guns N' Roses) • Wonderwall (Oasis) • You Were Meant for Me (Jewel).

Book with Online Audio & Video
00152225 .... $17.99

"CROSSROADS" & 9 MORE BLUES CLASSICS

Born Under a Bad Sign Albert King) • Cross Road Blues (Crossroads) (Cream) • Hide Away (Freddie King) • I'm Tore Down (Eric Clapton) • I'm Your Hoochie Coochie Man (Muddy Waters) • Killing Floor (Howlin' Wolf) • Mary Had a Little Lamb (Buddy Guy) • Still Got the Blues (Gary Moore) • Texas Flood (Stevie Ray Vaughan and Double Trouble) • The Thrill Is Gone (B.B. King).

Book with Online Audio & Video
00152183 .... $17.99

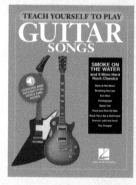

"SMOKE ON THE WATER" & 9 MORE HARD ROCK CLASSICS

Bark at the Moon (Ozzy Osbourne) • Breaking the Law (Judas Priest) • Iron Man (Black Sabbath) • Photograph (Def Leppard) • Rebel Yell (Billy Idol) • Rock and Roll All Nite (KISS) • Rock You like a Hurricane (Scorpions) • Runnin' with the Devil (Van Halen) • Smoke on the Water (Deep Purple) • The Trooper (Iron Maiden).

Book with Online Audio & Video
00152230 .... $17.99

"DUST IN THE WIND" & 9 MORE FINGERPICKING CLASSICS

Anji (Simon & Garfunkel) • Babe, I'm Gonna Leave You (Led Zeppelin) • Blackbird (The Beatles) • Dee (Randy Rhoads) • Dust in the Wind (Kansas) • Fire and Rain (James Taylor) • Little Martha (The Allman Brothers Band) • Take Me Home, Country Roads (John Denver) • Tears in Heaven (Eric Clapton) • Time in a Bottle (Jim Croce).

Book with Online Audio & Video
00152184 .... $17.99

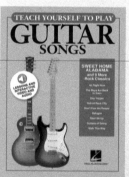

"SWEET HOME ALABAMA" & 9 MORE ROCK CLASSICS

All Right Now (Free) • The Boys Are Back in Town (Thin Lizzy) • Day Tripper (The Beatles) • Detroit Rock City (KISS) • Don't Fear the Reaper (Blue Oyster Cult) • Refugee (Tom Petty and the Heartbreakers) • Start Me Up (The Rolling Stones) • Sultans of Swing (Dire Straits) • Sweet Home Alabama (Lynyrd Skynyrd) • Walk This Way (Aerosmith).

Book with Online Audio & Video
00152181 .... $17.99

Each song includes online video lesson!

HAL•LEONARD® CORPORATION

7777 W. BLUEMOUND RD. P.O. BOX 13819 MILWAUKEE, WI 53213

www.halleonard.com

Prices, content and availability subject to change without notice.

0516